Percussion

Wendy Lynch

Heinemann Library
Chicago, Illinois

© 2002 Reed Educational & Professional Publishing
Published by Heinemann Library,
an imprint of Reed Educational & Professional Publishing,
Chicago, Illinois

Customer Service 888-454-2279

Visit our website at www.heinemannlibrary.com

Designed by Visual Image
Illustration by Jane Wakins
Originated by Dot Gradations
Printed and bound in South China

06 05 04 03 02
10 9 8 7 6 5 4 3 2 1

Library of Congress Cataloging-in-Publication Data
Lynch, Wendy, 1945-
     Percussion / Wendy Lynch.
       p. cm. -- (Musical instruments)
     Includes bibliographical references (p.   ) and index.
     ISBN 1-58810-235-1
     1. Percussion instruments--Juvenile literature. [1. Percussion
instruments.]   I. Title. II. Series.
   ML1030 .L96 2001
   786.8'19--dc21

                              2001000078

Acknowledgments
The publishers would like to thank the following for permission to reproduce photographs: pp. 4, 15, 20 Pictor; p. 5 Rex; pp. 6, 7, 12 Photodisc; p. 8 Andrew Lepley/Redferns; p. 9 David Toase/Travel Ink; p. 11 G. Salter/Lebrecht collection; pp. 13, 25 David Redfern/Redferns; pp. 14, 19 Chris Stock/Lebrecht collection; pp. 16, 24, 28, 29 Gareth Boden; pp. 17, 18 Sally Greenhill; p. 21 Corbis; p. 22 Ian Berry/Magnum; p. 23 Robert Harding; p. 26 Leon Morris/Redferns; p. 27 Mick Hutson/Redferns.

Cover photograph reproduced with permission of Photodisc.

Special thanks to Susan Lerner for her comments in the preparation of this book.

Every effort has been made to contact copyright holders of any material reproduced in this book. Any omissions will be rectified in subsequent printings if notice is given to the publisher.

Some words are shown in bold, **like this.** You can find out what they mean by looking in the glossary.

Contents

Making Music Together

There are many musical instruments in the world. Each instrument makes a different sound. We can make music together by playing these instruments in a band or an **orchestra.**

Bands and orchestras are made up of different groups of instruments. One of these groups is called percussion. In this **steel** band, everyone is playing a percussion instrument.

What Are Percussion Instruments?

There are many different kinds of percussion instruments. Each makes its own sound. Drums beat, cymbals crash, and tambourines jingle.

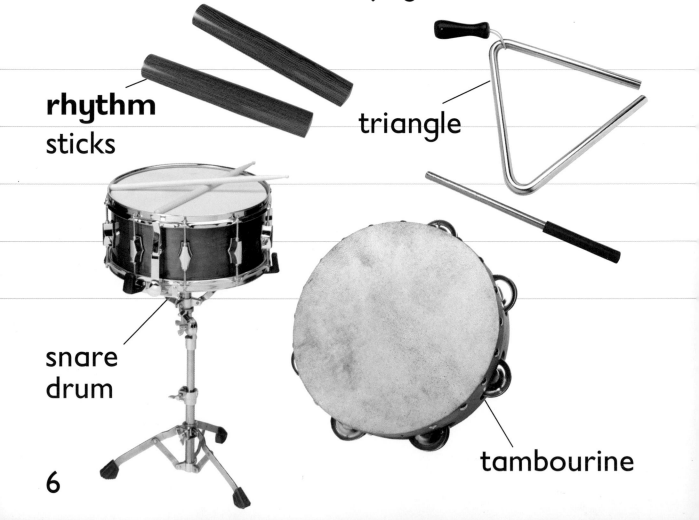

rhythm sticks

triangle

snare drum

tambourine

You bang, shake, or scrape percussion instruments to make a sound. They must be made of strong materials like gold, **steel, bronze,** or wood.

castanets

maracas

sleigh
bells

xylophone

Drums

Some kinds of drums are played with sticks. You can tap these bongo drums with your fingers or the heels of your hands. The pattern of short and long sounds you play is called a **rhythm.**

You can also play drums with other instruments in a band or an **orchestra.** The drums tap out a rhythm, keeping the beat for the other instruments in the orchestra or band.

How the Sound Is Made

You strike the **head,** or top, of a drum to make a sound. The head moves, making the air inside the drum move too. This movement is called vibration. When the air **vibrates,** it makes a sound.

When these two metal disks, called cymbals, hit against one another, the crash makes the metal vibrate. Big vibrations make a loud, low sound. Small vibrations make a soft sound.

Making a Sound

The **head** of a drum can be made of animal skin or plastic. Some drums make the same sound all the time, but you can change the sound in others.

A drum's sound, or **pitch,** can be high or low. Pressing a foot pedal changes the pitch for some drums. You **tighten** screws that tighten the head to change the pitch for others.

Types of Drums

Not all drums are the same. The bass drum is the biggest, so it plays the lowest and loudest notes. The snare drum has wires under the skin that rattle when you hit the drum.

Steel drums are made from oil barrels. Hitting the top in different places will change the sound. These metal drums sound very different from other drums.

Triangles and Xylophones

The triangle is a percussion instrument. You tap the triangle with a small rod to make a high, ringing sound. The note you play on the triangle is always the same.

The xylophone has wooden bars set on a frame. Each bar plays a different note when you tap it with a **mallet.** Some xylophones have a **hollow** wooden sound box under the bars.

The Percussion Section

In school, you may learn to play other percussion instruments. Some popular ones are chimes, maracas, **rhythm** sticks, and tambourines.

Some percussion instruments, like the triangle, are untuned. They play the same **pitch** all the time. Other percussion instruments are tuned, like tubular bells. They make many pitches.

The Wider Family

Castanets are made of two pieces of wood tied on a cord. You click the wooden disks together to make a sound. Dancers in Spain use castanets to make a **rhythm** for their dances.

The tambourine has pairs of small metal disks in its side. When you shake the tambourine or beat it with your hand, you can hear the discs jingle together.

Around the World

You can find percussion instruments all over the world. The talking drum, from Africa, can be used to send messages. Its strong sound can travel across long distances and even through forests.

The bonang is a set of gongs. It comes from Indonesia. You can hear the bonang and many other percussion instruments in a **gamelan orchestra.**

Famous Musicians and Composers

The **composer** Franz Joseph Haydn wrote the "Surprise Symphony." The surprise comes when you hear very loud drumbeats after some quiet music.

Today, you can hear Evelyn Glennie play percussion instruments. Evelyn is **deaf,** but she can feel the **vibration** of the music as she plays.

Percussion Music Today

You can hear percussion instruments in **jazz** and **rock** bands today. A set of drums called a drum kit is important in **pop** music. Its steady beat helps people to dance in time to the music.

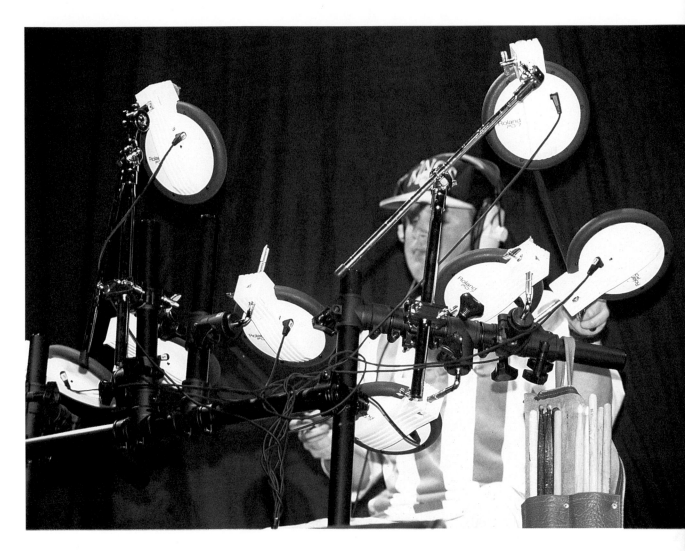

You can also make the sounds of drums with an electronic drum kit. When you hit the pad of a drum, it sends an electronic **pulse** to a control unit. This control unit plays the sound of the drum.

Sound Activities

You can make your own percussion instruments. Put some uncooked rice in an empty plastic cup. Put another empty cup on top and tape them together. Shake your shaker to make a **rhythm.**

You can make a xylophone. Line up six glass bottles or drinking glasses. Put a different amount of water in each. Tap them with a stick or spoon. Which sounds highest? Can you play a tune?

Thinking about Percussion

You can find the answers to all of these questions in this book.

1. What are some ways to play percussion instruments?

2. How can you change the **pitch** a drum plays?

3. Which drum plays the lowest, loudest notes?

4. What is the difference between tuned and untuned percussion instruments?

5. What is a bonang?

Glossary

bronze strong metal made up of copper and tin

composer person who writes music

deaf unable to hear

gamelan orchestra orchestra from Indonesia that includes many types of percussion instruments

head top of a drum

hollow empty inside

jazz style of music that is often made up as it is played

mallet small hammer with a rounded head and a long handle, used for playing some musical instruments

orchestra large group of musicians who play their instruments together

pitch highness or lowness of a sound or musical note

pop popular music

pulse single beat

rhythm pattern of repeated beats or sounds

rock kind of pop music with a strong beat

steel strong metal made of iron mixed with carbon

tighten to make tighter or more close-fitting

vibrate to move up or down or from side to side very quickly

More Books to Read

Kalman, Bobbie. *Musical Instruments from A to Z.* New York: Crabtree Publishing Company, 1997.

O'Brien, E. *Drums.* Tulsa, Okla.: EDC Publishing, 1998.

Turner, Barrie. *Percussion.* North Mankato, Minn.: Smart Apple Media, 1998.

Index